Nigel Pearce Selected Work

Nigel Pearce

chipmunkapublishing
the mental health publisher

Nigel Pearce

All rights reserved, no part of this publication may be reproduced by any means, electronic, mechanical photocopying, documentary, film or in any other format without prior written permission of the publisher.

>Published by
>Chipmunkapublishing
>United Kingdom

http://www.chipmunkapublishing.com

Copyright © 2017 Nigel Pearce

ISBN   978-1-78382-334-5

Author biography.

Nigel was born in 1959 and has experienced a colourful life which illustrated a lack of adequate 'socialization' from an early age, that is, for a variety of reasons and potential unreason he was not programmed by the what Louis Althusser called the Ideological State Apparatus. This lead him to run away from a complex home situation at twelve to the counter-culture where he mixed with avant-garde people of many beliefs. He was taken into the care of the County Council and transferred to the psychiatric system. He had experienced enforced medication and E.C.T.by the age of sixteen. After discovering academia and later Chipmunkapublishing. this is his ninth book with them, the direction of his life changed. Nigel was cured of a physical condition by a remarkable consultant and team at a local hospital and he has a second chance. He has been 'Clean and Dry' for over thirty years and is very pleased to be. Nigel has gained two Bachelor's Degrees one with Creative Writing and both 2/1s. He is at present engaged on the Masters Programme in English at the Open University.

Nigel Pearce

Nigel Pearce Selected Work

Introduction.

This collection of poetry, prose-fiction and non-fiction traversers a wide range from poetry inspired from memories in the last of the old asylums he lived in and out of too ruminations on Antigone and from poetic and fictional accounts of various descents into ill health as well as speculations on how we all need a healthier way of life. It is a mixed bag, so get reading and hang on to your flying goggles.

Nigel Pearce

Nigel Pearce Selected Work

Contents:

Part One Poetry.
Pages: 5-27

Part Two Prose fiction.
Pages: 28-40

Part Three Other Prose.
Pages 42-112.

Nigel Pearce

Nigel Pearce Selected Work

**Part One:
Poetry**

Nigel Pearce

Memories of Central Hospital.

The house on a high hill, with wandering grounds of green
Where Summer's rays caressed the patients,
Who stretched upon abundant lawns,
Clothes that did not fit their bodies,
While nurses watched with nodding approval,
With an endless stream of coffee and ego,
White-coated doctors cruised around the wards,
Like spiritual directors in a religious community,
They roared with potency,
And wept with fallibility.
Windows which did not open,
Prevented leaps of freedom,
Shiny white tablets shaped like flying-saucers,
For those who dreamt beyond the horizon,
And chalky yellow pills for those trapped,
Within a marsh and seeking salvation,
For all the wobbling souls within that red, bricked house,
Which bobbed like a shop on the cruel sea,
Surrounded by the icy stares of ivy choked outsiders.

Nigel Pearce

Group Therapy

Crawling painfully as on broken glass,
Your eyes flickering with eternity,
Contorted by creeping coffin aches.

Flaming anger at a myriad wrongs,
Your parents, husband, wife, baby or cult,
They parade for an inspection
   with you crucified before them.

My enfeebled vision tossed by this tempest,
Love wrecked on the shores
   of this interminable scream,
Which echoes across a desert
   whipped by wind.

A desert where most reside,
Blind to my pleas,
You tear yourself crawling
   while they sleep.

"Hello"

Wandering wondering through
    your colour spectrum,
Which as seasons passing
    lament the Dead,
The corpses of the forgotten
    lovers weep,
We are harvested by a
    scythe of undulating light.

Harvested one cider evening,
As our chaff blinds the Dead,
And our fertility nurtures the
    Living,
Embraced by the eternal roaming
    of Light and Dark.

Laughing at those ensnared by
    twilight's mute labyrinth,
Isis casts our dust upon the
    Nile,
Only to be transfigured by
    it's motion,
To enrich the barren shores
    at flood.

We are dust and water,
Blood from Mother Isis,
Tears from the crucified Zealot
Invigorated like a leaf
    on a swift breeze.

For we dared to dance,
Upon the barricades of
    black smoke tyres,
With the banner soaked with
    Isis' blood,
We, martyred by the freeze,
    now adsolved by History.

Nigel Pearce

"Good-bye"

Damned by dazzling Destiny,
Which cut like crimson
    blade,
Lunged at by day-light
    death-dream,
Ripping his entrails like a
    filtered fish.

Damned by dazzling Destiny,
His poetry torn by Fate's
    claws,
She perceived only parchment
    muddle,
Only to wonder who and
    why?

Damned by dazzling
    Destiny,
The mystic sunk from an
    unknowing cloud,
Like a stone ripples a
    pond,
The pulsating water like
    a baptism.

Damned by dazzling
    Destiny,
His burden scented with
    lavender
Upon which the pyre of
    Fate burnt,
Like purgatory's fire consumed
    Destiny's snare.

Our Lightness is Their Darkness

Wailing from the depths of the mass mound grave,
Where the waking dead were thrown like Mozart,
Maggots feasting on flesh and eye,
No tomb visitors except Sunday asylum callers.

Now community care cast away
The tooth comb lawns,
Tea and cheese wedges of brake
With the passing of the seasons
No longer the long timers lying on verdant pasture
But, the anonymous managers with blank expressions.

They consider: "Will anyone chisel out concrete eyes?"
If we cast the ashes to the whirling winds,
Who will chase the winter chill down,
As frost-ice evaporates dripping into grey slush.

And the howl wind tempest of ash,
Now transfigured into a Temple for those,
Who like the rise and setting of the sun,
Know that only summers bring insanity: the winter death
Reason.

And we know that insanity is sanity
And our Light is their Darkness.

Nigel Pearce

Tadpole In A Jam Jar

The wind blew through hospital grounds,
Where strolling patients and curious nurses
Wandered.

The cardboard in which he lived,
Had been soaked by a whistling storm,
The fierce rain had saturated
The papier mache box of being,
The sodden paper had sagged,
And slopped into a wallpaper droop,
On the admission ward floor.

Some tried to swab the gash,
Others wiped their feet in the wound,
While most merely observed him;
As a schoolboy watched
A tadpole in a jam jar.

A cloud embraced the aching
like an ember which pulsates
        with a warmth
Her rain caressed frozen field,
extinguish
       a
          solitary
                candle.
Sun strokes like the morning
We are the dance of shadows
some eyes are burnt our loss
Dry a tear of noon like a tide.

On Poetry
sweetest tears are wept;
Caressing the shadows of silence
this Muse is ancient as Electra;

She whispers breath onto a
tissue psyche,
Which vibrates like a web
of gossamer:

Dream with shifting sands
like a vortex of voids.

Doves with broken wings
who fly from a cage,
Scribe those poems of Night
which ache with love's sorrow.

Nigel Pearce Selected Work

Lines Written upon Hearing Voices

He was like carrion on
    the wasteland,
With vultures ripping his
    flesh from his soul,
Desert sand stinging his
    Eyes like salt in a wound,
And the desert is reflected
    in his mind.

Those bitter voices burning
    likening scolding water,
Ached like the pain
    crossing his mind,
Like a metamorphosis
    fertility became fallow,
Like the twilight proceeds
    that bitter-sweet night.

His muse, emaciated, claws
    the labyrinth of his mind,
To awaken him from his
    reverie,
She massages the thoughts
    of his tempest torn soul,
And he gradually stumbles
    towards an oasis.

Nigel Pearce

<u>Romeo and Juliet</u>

Spring aches in their heart of embers, serpents do glide the Time,
The apple blossom is impregnated artificially with resin at dawn,
Do silicone petals have the thirst for sun the organic one's claim,
the world is transmogrified it is no longer carbon based, concrete,
Trees of luminous green rubber are still sensitive to humus touch,
Touch, Midas touch, no gold finger is on the run from the masses.

Children of eve far to early we know the polar melts before sunset,
Ice melts in a deluge, hurricanes howl across star-crossed lovers,
 revaluation. no, Juliet had raided the Friar Lawrence's DDA box,
The planets rotate in a different way today, tides of lover's crash.
The poet koows the curse of the elders is chisselled in stone,
The sage can hand a phial to numb the pain or blood to write.

Visiting mother.

The house on a bourgeois terrace,
Converted from delicate manners
And repressed emotions
Into a rambling corridor place,
I gaze at this old lady
Who has insect thin frail arms,
And wonder,
Do not comprehend,
Cannot respond
To her incoherent
Dreamy nightmare
Emptiness

You are not
The dancing soul
Woman I knew;
A delicate, crunched shell
You stand wobbling,
For your final fall
Is in immediate
Weeping tomorrows.

Perhaps
Your sunset
Will bring comforting nights.

Nigel Pearce

Narodnik in 1985.

Misfortune struck like being beheaded because of a Yankee War,
Neither clean or dry but not H. I V. as tested down London in 1985,
Those miners had been fighting and loosing for a year, strike in the
Belly of the beast with a thunder bolt: Angry Brigade 2, emerald cell,
We had the reverie and blurry plots, they had the guns and Semtex,
Six months then we see the quarter-master says, 'drugs are no-go'.

Mugged by the plain clothes, Seven Sisters Road but not for drugs,
The guardians of the state were waiting walloped spread eagled mc;
I had been losing sanity like a melting glacier now it had evaporated,
Whisked away 'chasing' and 'chipping' in ALF not very 'safe houses',
I was sheltered until the worms ate my mind, political asylum in a bin
Lost like a rainbow in the midnight of their souls, I kept my eyes shut.

The anti-terrorist squad shoot first now, suicide was never our aim.

The Deception of Psychiatry.

A Sappho who refuses to be a poet and lesbian,
She is a weaver of words "homophobic lesbian",
Sadly, she sought out both lunacy and asylums,
Admission, soaked up symptoms with sponges,
Took decades to penetrate that cloud of knowing,
In an attic, not Bertha Masan yet still strange brew.

This poetess bewitched me amongst some others,
Now the shrinks and staff look stupid and resent it,
They have cobbled together OCD, PD, depression,
She spent decades in hospitals, 'love in the asylum',
For me she was Maud Gonne, an intelligent beauty,
Wrote poems for her she wants to stay in The Maze.

A woman who did think she really was Maud Gonne,
Caught the ferry from Holyhead in 1981 disappeared,
Her face lingers in me still she, dreamer of absolutes,
Degree of abstraction, First in Literature evaded a net,
You were lost in ideas, books, folklore, another cause,
Shelley, Elanor Marx, Padraig Pearse, Sands, Yeats,
 You did look like Maud Gonne, perhaps you were her?

Nigel Pearce

<u>Winter Poem #5</u>

She had so loved that summer as the sun savoured her skin,
A burning disc had also burnt like a rapture in her mind's eye,
We were bidding farewell as the gold cloak of Autumn spread,
As lovers of the seasons we must move with a cycle of moons.

A winter ice tore jabbed and speared his heart without mercy,
No number of wool blankets would protect against that freeze,
He could not exorcise with bell and Bible a glacier that clawed,
Did the solution lie in a bottle of whisky a warm shot of smack?

No! Because that Spring he had been cured of a deadly disease,
A solution is drawn up into a pen he writes across a naked page,
The words which are wonders as they warm a chilly Winter's day,
He closes that book and finds solace and shelter in the chapters.

A poem upon reading Rosa Luxemburg #3.

5 March 1871 – 15 January 1919.

"War unleashes – at the same time as the reactionary forces of the capitalist
world – the generating forces of social revolution which ferment in its depths."

- Rosa Luxemburg.

You were human far too human to fasten their door with wooden bolt,
Rosa of flowers, of the sketchpad, of the poem, of the theoretical tone,
Of the blood connected with veins to that beating heart of the masses.

Rosa of the prison cell as your analysis *The Accumulation of Capital*,
Explained why the fields of Europe were sodden with worker's blood,
You were no pacifist but took your logic to its conclusion incarceration.
When the war transmuted into revolutions and mutinies you seized the
scorching red rod of History
With bare hands and believed now was the time of Capital's graveyard,
Then chaos and mayhem an 'Unanswered Question' of a red vanguard,
I know as the reactionary's rifle butt smashed your skull you spat at him.

Red Rosa, you were *the living flame of revolution* said Clara Zeitlin,

Nigel Pearce

Yet she would trundle into a mausoleum when
ordered to condemn
your anti-Leninist deviations
by the Comintern after Vladimir Lenin
was mummified by Joe Stalin.

The flickering flame of red revolution must be
rekindled today for as
you said there is a choice:
"Socialism or Barbarism."

The Banker and his maladies.

He barks and howls his orders like steel bullets,
But vestments of Capital suit with tie are twisted,
He is a sly priest enrobed just another Pharisee,
He sighs with a pleated moan at cocktail parties,
Then captains a yacht in seas of fictitious dollars.

But beware you are no mirage grey anachronism,
The lava of the oppressed is bubbling up red hot,
It will sweep dust out of your empty opera houses,
Bourgeois the cardboard ballet with a cut-out ends,
Tremble and dance to a terrible toll of a Death Bell.

It rings in their ears so they wince whine and weep,
The proletariat strikes, a black panther on the prey.

Nigel Pearce

The Cube.

My name is Nikolai and I address you from a
ward in the asylum.
I was merely sitting huddled in an overcoat
observing a light bulb.
It is suspended, like my mind, by a single cord.
It begins pulsating slightly or so it seems.
No, it is the bulb that flickers.
This room is like a cube of pure white
Which is caressed by fingers of both light
and dark.
A pixilated light begins to merge into a dawn
Which is peeping through the curtains.
They are made of yellow lace
And hang on steel wires that are suspended
between two hooks.
Finding my feet and gliding around the bulb
To discover a yellowish square of plastic.
I locate a switch and click it off,
The bulb is extinguished and so is my mind,
It is cast into an ocean of crawling patterns
That dissolve into mirrors of wax.
Locate the switch again and push the button on
So, the electricity dazzles this cube.
It bounces off these walls of white and drowns me.
A morning lurks outside the room
And it is a world of twisting serpents
With eyes of composite deception.
A big polished black boot kicks open the door
And crushes me as if I were a piece of origami.
There is also sleet outside
That burns like the Sulphur of Hell.
It is finger-numbingly cold in their inferno.
They may believe I have a torn and twisted heart.

It is neither cold nor black,
But rather it is red and had just beaten too hard.
I run from the room and feel like water spurting from a geyser
And then fall to Earth with a splat
And am instantaneously frozen.
I was in no doubt their hearts were true blue
And cold like the sky hanging across Antarctica.
My heart has been forcibly frozen!
It's like a steel arrow
And once placed in a crossbow can pierce the coldest soul in rusty armour.
When blue souls are haemorrhaged by this bolt,
There is nothing.
Only a foul smell of decay in a wilderness
Which will be blown away by the wind.

Nigel Pearce

On the nature of Idols #3.

> *'Andrea: Unhappy is the land that breeds no hero.*
>
> *Galileo: No, Andrea: Unhappy is the land that needs a hero.'*
>
> - Bertolt Brecht, *Life of Galileo* (1938), Scene 12, p. 115.

A beaver just slipped into a river's current flowing,
She seemed so soft swift and was brown in colour,
The water had glistened and rippled with pleasure,
Her dive was deep to delve in the enigmas hidden,
The fur wild and remained untamed, here is no pet.

I watched dark with praise yet carried along a way,
Possessed with fire was burnt until the poem wrote,
Every day I wander to the river and admire an idol,
Strung-out, I sneak a shot from that Pantheist bible.

One day a beaver will dive with me and we will fly,
A harmony of humans and heroes will touch a sky,
That wet dewy morning, no one will need to weep,
For we will then all be free from bonds of hierarchy

Nigel Pearce Selected Work

Nigel Pearce

On smoking the homegrown of people in authority.

They were of different ideas spheres of persuasion,
The youngsters were stimulated with a flip into an Arctic sea of submerged icebergs and lost albatross,
no physical contact just the deep freeze.

We would experience the dark night of the soul or
An existential crisis depending on who rolls a dice,
There were the respective intelligentsia whom one pleased in separate rooms with gymnastics.

But we were on the second story, above an attic
Where secreted sequestered was amphetamine
In plenty snorted off a Steely Dan album shelve,
no mooring there or here, we were adrift.

Dutifully reading *Borstal Boy* as it was mandatory,
One arrived and the trendies genuflect, those fools.
Off to different congresses and seminars; anarchy,
sweet marijuana weed from a garden
was smoked.

Nigel Pearce Selected Work

Nigel Pearce

Nigel Pearce Selected Work

Part 2.
Prose Fiction

Nigel Pearce

Easter

And what excess of love
bewildered them till they died?
I write it out in verse-
MacDonald and MacBride
And Connelly and Pearse
Now and in time to be,
Whenever green is worn,
Are changed, changed utterly:
A terrible beauty is born.
- W.B. Yeats
Easter 1916. [extract] (1988) pp 296-29.

You may wonder what I was doing in Finsbury Park. We Catholics are indeed everywhere we are ubiquitous. Here in England many think of us as almost like dirty pests. Although we had always observed their behaviour with interest and often alarm. We had always travelled light and took notes on those who regarded us as parasites. This is my tale, the tale of an everyday Mary. A woman who had a variety of Holy statues in her flat: The Sacred Heart of Jesus, Our Lady Immaculate and lived with her teenage son. I am a trinity: a single mother, my son and that echo in my mind which is my father who had seen the inside of the H-Blocks.

Nigel Pearce

A gust of cold wind whirled into my small council flat in North London and I shivered as I saw a faint spectral almost undefinable figure hover briefly above my Holy statues. These broken windows were becoming a problem; the neighbours were gossiping; the social worker was becoming suspicious and simply the price of paying the glazier was becoming a task. I had many tribulations and the consensus woven into the local fabric was that they mainly emanated from Joseph, my son. People said it was a little more than the usual growing pains all teenagers are stung with when they stumble into that hornet's nest of metamorphosis called adolescence. I swept up the slivers of glass and called a glazier who I did business with yet again. There was no question of a call to the council for repairs as they had begun asking awkward questions. He replaced the window, puttied it in and said:

'I hope you don't mind me saying this but it is costing you a fortune Mary.

You must be pleased I did the job on the cheap.'

I tried not to grimace lowering a veil
of lace and then replied:

'And I hope you would not be
concerned if I said that it helps keep
you in business, Mr O'Connor. The
reasons I ring you are purely one's
of business not social work, you
understand.'

'Alright, alright. I was only trying to
help.'

He huffed and puffed out and
slammed the front door. I noted a
swagger in his walk. Maybe he
thought himself better or was he
afraid of the supposedly
unpredictable behaviour of those
who lived in our area. Or he could be
undercover?

Fidgeting more than usual when my
eyes noticed what the time was. I
wondered where my son had got to
and then as if by synchronicity he
erupted into the room:
'Where have you been?'

'Hi yeah mum, I was only at the
Mosque.'

'Now what is a Catholic boy doing in
a Mosque? That is not to say I am

against interfaith relations. That one has got a bit of a reputation now in Finsbury Park and with the Brits generally. I have heard they have been some quite extreme preachers there:

'They are not called preachers, but Imams. Mother.'

'Alright, but be careful Joe. I don't want a convert on my hands as that would take some explaining.'

We smiled at each other in a pact of reassurance; pacts lead to the signing of

Treaties and we both knew a Treaty is not worth the paper or ink.

    I had been going to Mass on a more regular footing since the windows had been smashed and replaced so many times. What I could not ascertain was why they were being bricked. Some local people knew my father had been in "the 'army', the 'Provo's" during the war in the North and had done time in 'The Maze'. That was why I had left, well sort of anyway. There is a grapevine you would only understand if you came from a Republican family. It spreads in two ways, both in the community and to the Brits. I knew it had been a mistake to attend that meeting to set up a steering committee for an event to mark the centenary. One hundred years since Easter 1916 and the blood sacrifice of Connolly, Pearse, MacBride and others. I had been taught to recite Padraig Parse's last words at his execution before I could read and became lost in clouds condensed from memory and reverie which then rained words:

"The fools, the fools! - They have left us our Finnian dead, and while Ireland holds these graves, Ireland unfree shall never be at peace."

I had not noticed that Joe had buzzed backed into the front room where I had remained after he stomped off to his bedroom:

'Stop it, stop that bloody crap mum. We both know that you were tar-and-feathered when you got pregnant the first time. Whatever happened to the child mother? Was it a boy or a girl? Eh!'

Joseph screamed and sobbed simultaneously.

Nigel Pearce

'Mary, Mother of God, I swear those words just came out Joseph.'

I said this in a measured voice which was a method learnt as a child. Joe had become just like my father in some ways, but he had no cause and would not have had the discipline to fight for one if he did I guessed, I believed.

Easter came and went with a slightly increased dissident Republican activity in the North, but nothing that my father would have considered sufficient to rouse sleeping Eire. I now know for certain the War was over. If the dissidents couldn't orchestrate a couple of spectaculars and the masses was quiescence on the centenary of the blood sacrifice of Easter 1916. It really was finished. The truth slapped me in the face as brutally as any R.U.C officer had done to generations of Catholic women. Maybe it was just as well Sinn Féin had adopted a Pan-Nationalist electoral policy which may create a United Ireland eventually, an Irish Workers Socialist Republic I now very much doubted. That apparition appeared before me a second time. This time it was possible to perceive some of its features. It was a shimmer that was both pale and emaciated with long dark hair. I kept these matters to myself because I had an aunt who was detained in Manchester under the Mental Health Act on Section 2 and was in the language of her doctors:

        Migrated to Section 3 so we can make sure she has the full range of therapeutic interventions for her benefit. Another letter had said she was forced to have medication and that made me shudder more than any ghost could have done.

    Joe had departed from the house and a silence as dense as crystal filled the void. I repressed thoughts of his father. Though I was becoming concerned about Joseph's increasing interest in a politicized version of a very fundamentalist Islam. It was beginning to dominate him. I was opposed to this on two levels. Firstly, there was the question of Roman Catholicism and secondly, that of the potential for violence and wrongheaded violence at that. It seemed my father's activity had been justified. But to get involved with that group who may well have been originally a Frankenstein created by the West. It was heresy politically and they were really an apocalyptic cult. This was a qualitatively different situation to what had existed in Ireland and I had to draw a line. The line was soon crossed! The police arrived, they knew me or at least of me and my background. Joe had been arrested and was being questioned about 'conspiring with others to prepare for an act of terrorism.' Although as the conversation developed I ascertained he hadn't yet been charged.

'Hail Mary, full of grace, pray for us sinners, now and at the hour of our death'.

I said with a stony silence. It had become a pre-recorded response of Irish Catholics in these situations. A forty-eight-hour order was extended by the Home Sectary to twenty-eight days. No one in the official or unofficial Republican movement would sully their hands with this one. I was told in the deep recesses of an anonymous pub:

'It would not be in the wider interests of building momentum in the rank and file towards an end game of Irish Emancipation.'

So, my son who is the teenage grandchild of a man who

had been subjected to the horrors of the H-Blocks was now expendable because he had an inconvenient ideology'

'There would be no legal assistance. The decision has been made by the Army Council who as you have always known Mary is the legitimate government of Ireland being the direct inheritors of the authority of Dáil Éireann.'

'A question of bloody 'Ecco Homo'[1] more like.'

It was a dark, very bleak and wet journey back to Finsbury Park. When I reached home, I arrived drenched by the cold rain and threw myself onto my bed without changing my sodden clothes. Whether I developed a fever I shall never know. A third apparition came towards me. This time there was no mistaking the figure, it was Bobby Sands, the first hunger striker to die in 1981 a poet and an elected M.P.

---

[1] In the Vulgate Bible, the Latin phrase: 'Ecco Homo' or 'Behold the human' is said by Pontius Pilate as he washes his hands to free himself of guilt for the crucifixion of Jesus of Nazareth.

Nigel Pearce

His life and poetry were familiar to me; he had the status of a secular saint in Republican circles and beyond. He said tenderly:

'Mary, do you understand now W. B. Yeats was correct when he wrote in his poem *Easter 1916*: "Too long a sacrifice/Can make a stone of the heart"

I awoke in a fever and my clothes were soaked with sweat and I knew my life had been irrevocably changed. Fortunately, Joe was released without charge as the evidence would not have stood in court. It was flimsy and circumstantial. A few weeks later in the afternoon we received a surprise visit from Mr. O'Connor. To his astonishment, I immediately welcomed him into our little concrete nest. He sat down and without hesitation begun:

'This may come as a quite a shock to you. I am your uncle, your father's brother. He was killed on 'active service' and that is all you need to know. It is the Veterans branch of Sinn Fenn that now preserves Ireland's cultural heritage since the

Good Friday Agreement, you understand?'

'Yes, yes of course.'

'They have bought you, Joe and someone Joe has never met. A young woman you last saw as a new-born.'

Joe exclaimed:

'There was no abortion?!'

O'Connor continued:

'They have bought a cottage in the rural West for the three of you. You will never 'want for anything."'

'Joe, it looks like you have a family after all.' I said.

'And perhaps we all have a future.' He replied.

Some reflections on the short-story: *Easter.*

In *Easter* I attempted a traditional short story. An *exposition that* introduced Mary and Joseph, their setting implied a theme and foreshadows the story. It creates the circumstances for the *inciting moment* that through a series of *causes and effects* propelled by *external* and *internal conflicts* until the story reached its *climax*. This created the conditions for the *reversal* in my protagonist and subsequent *transformation* in character and circumstance. That had a causal relationship to increasing weighted *effects* resolved in the *denouement.* The latter is followed by a Chekhovian Ending. It is written in First person POV [point of view] and the genre is Realism/Family Saga. I attempted to use Aristotelian *poetics* as shown by Freytag below:

Nigel Pearce

Haunting Hardy.

Emily wondered about Thomas. It could have been that Kitchener-like moustache. No, surely it was all much closer to home that. You had promised and vowed to nurture both my writing and my life. But you were just swollen like an over-ripened peach with fame, she thought. Emily had married him and was flipped into a goldfish bowl. I was never any more than your secretary. Emily, felt she had just been a literary mirror of his full portrait. No doubt he had written great novels, Tess and Jude. Now Emily haunted him in the corridors of academia. She thought, Jude Fowley had an eye for books and a mind like a verdant pasture in which he had hoped to cultivate the loftiest of ideas. He believed the gowned ones at Christ minister to be eagles. Yet they would become the vultures who would peck at the corpses of his children. Emily had also read his poem Mad Judy, and thought, it caught the growl and howl of his Thanatos bellow. Mad Judy had bewailed the birth of children as: 'more comers to this stony shore.' Then Emily decided to rattle her chains upon Thomas' bejewelled coffin and all she heard was a disembodied voice reply, 'Hello dear, it is time for afternoon tea.'
That encapsulates him, Emily thought. Emily awaited the night and the moon which her muse because it illuminated her haunting hour. And then, like Lady Lazarus, she would arise.

Nigel Pearce Selected Work

**Part Three.
Other Prose.**

Nigel Pearce

On Antigone.

This thesis will endeavour to show the debates between Antigone and Creon continued across texts and modes of production. They indeed must until the material conditions which gave rise to them are resolved as Louis MacNeice suggested in the second dawn of civilisation:

Communism in its truest sense is an effort to think, and to think into
action human society as an organism[2].

Hegel described *Antigone* from a bourgeois dialectical position as 'celestial Antigone[3]' representing the ruling class family, Creon as the antithesis, *polis* and a higher synthesis of family and *polis*. Marx turned Hegel's dialectic on its head, thus placing Hegel's aesthetics and dialectic in material reality. This is the methodology employed in my thesis. It is derived from Marx illustrated below in Jameson[4]

Superstructures		CULTURE IDEOLOGY (philosophy, religion, etc.) THE LEGAL SYSTEM POLITICAL SUPERSTRUCTURES AND THE STATE
Base or infrastructure	THE ECONOMIC, OR MODE OF PRODUCTION	RELATIONS OF PRODUCTION (classes) FORCES OF PRODUCTION (technology, ecology, population)

---

[2] *Louis MacNeice, Selected Literary Criticism*, ed. Alan Heuser (Oxford, Clarendon 1987), p.6.
[3] Bernstein, J..M, *Hegel's Feminism* [Ed] Fanny Söderbäck Feminist Readings of Antigone (SUNY series in Gender Theory, State University of New York Press, 2010). p.111.
[4] Fredric Jameson, *The Political Unconscious: Narrative as a socially symbolic act* (London, Routledge Classics, 2002) p. 17.

Hence, any Marxist critique relies on the existence of a material base to society that reflects culture, indeed, literature. However, I argue this is no one-way relation because the superstructure interacts back onto the base creating another dialectical relationship[5]. I think Caudwell was correct by suggesting:

What is the basis of literary art? What is the inner contradiction which produces its own onward movement?
Poetry is clotted social history, the emotional sweat of man's
struggle with Nature.'[6]
Thus, for this thesis, each manifestation of Antigone is based on 'clotted' or concrete moments which are dialectically posed. Nevertheless, Hellenistic Greece was a unique society. A direct democracy where the sacred was interwoven into everyday life. The Aristotelian structure of Greek tragedy as codified in Aristotle, *Poetics* [Fig 2 Freytag's Triangle] was integrated into this religious life:

---

[5] Paul Blackledge *Reflections on the Marxist theory of History* (Manchester, Manchester University Press, 2006) pp. 25-26
[6] Christopher Caudwell, *Illusion and Reality* (London, Lawrence & Wishart, 1946) p .130. p.201.

Nigel Pearce Selected Work

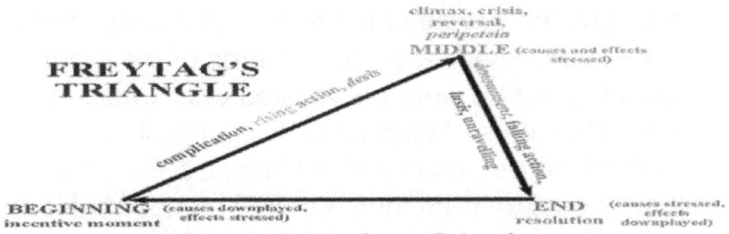

[7]

It is of significance that Aristotle thought *Oedipus Rex*, also written by Sophocles to be the perfect play because Aristotle argued it illustrated three essential elements 1) unity of action 2) unity of time: the action in a play should take place in the span of a day and a night (this is important because the Athenian theatre was open air and consequently, 3) unity of place. Inherent in Hellenistic poetics was the predetermination of the major characters who were 'heroes' from a 'cultural store' of myths which were reinterpreted by different authors. Hence, we can see how Sophocles used irony. In *Antigone,* the audience sees the denouement on stage, yet the philosophical or ideological questions remain. Also, Sophocles introduced 'the third person' on stage, so Antigone is in dialogue with Ismene at the beginning which adds an extra dimension to the performance. Sophocles' play won the competition at the festival of Dionysus in 441 B.C.,

---

[7]

http://gateway.proquest.com.libezproxy.open.ac.uk/openurl?ctx_ver=Z39.88-2003&xri:pqil:res_ver=0.2&res_id=xri:lion&rft_id=xri:lion:rec:ref:R04432121&rft.accountid=14697

and thus, he achieved fame as both a writer and a statesman. The first written records of the drama text of Antigone were not located until 1,500 years later. Problems of translation into English are evident by the period which elapsed before the first was taken from the Latin by Thomas Watson in 1581.

Evidence of the dialectical conflict between Creon and Antigone in dramaturgy, literature and philosophy can be in Steiner *Antigone*[8]. It is important, though, to note that the play was more nuanced than Creon simply as the antithesis of a revolutionary Antigone. Creon is transformed by *peripeteia* during the play, and Antigone takes her *physic* to its conclusion. Therefore, his defence of the *polis* changes over time in the context of a Hellenistic society which was a fusion of sacred and secular.:

The man who came to burn the pillars and treasures
of their temples, to burn their country and scatter its
laws to the winds? Can you see the gods honouring evil men?
Impossible!
Sophocles, L. 261-5.[9]
So, Creon acted on religiopolitical grounds. Antigone was motivated substantially by religious

---

[8] George Steiner, *The Antigone Myth in Western literature, Art and, Thought* (Oxford, Oxford University Press 2003).
[9] Sophocles, Antigone (trans) David Franklin and John Harrison, Cambridge, Cambridge University Press. L.261-5. 2003) Hereafter cited as Sophocles L.#.

purification and burial rites. The burial of Polyneices.

Steiner illustrated Antigone and Creon's dialectic in modernity by referencing Heinrich Boll's script which was used in the television series *Der Herbst in Deutschland* 1979[10] [The German Autumn] which explored the *Antigone* text and Marxism. I note that German audiences at that time would have been aware that the phrase 'German Autumn' referenced an attempt by the urban guerrilla group Red Army Faction/Socialist Patients Collective to topple the West German State. In this context, Ismene paradoxical imagery anticipated the play's conflicts

You have a *hot heart* for *chilling deeds*.[11] Sophocles.L88.

Jean Anouilh's play was written in 1942 during the Nazi occupation, and to the dismay of the Communist, Resistance performed in Paris, 1944. Camus noted in 1952 they were unhappy with its ramifications for the Vichy regime:

Antigone is right – but Creon is not wrong.
Anouilh *Antigone* p xiv[12]

In contrast to Sophocles, Anouilh employed the Prologue-Chorus, which was probably Anouilh's boldest innovation. As a single character who interacts with and comments on both the action and on the nature of drama, employing meta-

---

[10] George Steiner, *The Antigone Myth in Western literature, Art and, Thought* (Oxford, Oxford University Press 2003) p.p. 150-151, p.196.

[11] My italics.

[12] Jean Anouilh, *Antigone* (trans Barbara Bray, London Bloomsbury 2013). Hereafter referred cited Anouilh p #.

theatre. Alternatively, Sophocles had begun with two sisters speaking outside the city, i.e. the 'public sphere'. Anouilh commences with a man commenting on all members of the cast. We later hear a cry of desperation from him:

> Don't let her die Creon! We will all bear the scar for thousands of
> years.
>
> Anouilh p. 49

The chorus in Anouilh was aware of the conventions of tragedy and secularized the play. At the Premiere, in occupied Paris, he would know if Antigone was seen to die ignobly this would be a blow to the Resistance. However, Creon feared the 'mob' and despite the pleas from Haemon and the intervention of the Chorus he was ruthless in sacrificing Antigone to propitiate them. Here is an example of dramatic irony because intertextually the audience would have known the 'mob' were sympathetic to Antigone in Sophocles:

Chorus. Can't you try to gain time, and have her escape,
tomorrow.
Creon. The mob knows already. They're all around the
palace yelling. I can't turn back.
Anouilh p.50.

What strikes is the use of the vernacular.
Creon might be a personification of the State or in Nazi occupation as Father/ Fuhrer:
That **g**iant-**g**od.
Anouilh, p.51.
Alliterative '**g**'s in the 'target' translation:
Haemon (crying out like a child, throwing himself into Creon's arms)

Oh, Father, it isn't true, it isn't you, it isn't happening.
… I beg you to let me admire you still.
Anouilh p. 52
The line commenced with an apostrophe 'Oh' continued with anapaestic feet asking three rhetorical questions demanding paternal reassurance:
Creon (putting him away). You have looked up to your father too long. Look
me straight in the eye. That is what it means to be a man.
                                                    Anouilh p. 52.
This suggested a psychoanalytical moment which later manifested as an Oedipal Complex. Agreeing with Badiou that a Freudo-Marxist model with Creon perceived as a 'superego' had explanatory value:

Here in the counterpart of the superego is the fact that the essence
and the constitutive core of the State, the domination of one class by
another is always dictatorial.[13]
Creon's 'look me straight in the eyes' resounded intertextually with Harrison[14] whose gaze of the 20th century's elites looked upon the innocents of the world and petrified without pity. Harrison[15]:

---

[13] Alain Badiou *Theory of the Subject* (London, Continuum, 2009) p.159.
[14] Tony Harrison. *The Gaze of the Gorgon*. Newcastle-upon-Tyne: Bloodaxe Books, 1992, p. 64.
[15] ibid

Nigel Pearce

A verse commentary on the unspeakable horrors of the twentieth century:
what are we doing with our art?
are we still strumming the right lyre
to play us through the century's fire?
The rhyme of lyre and fire stressed the contradictory relationship between art and war. Creon was implacable:
Creon: She has spoken now. All Thebes knows what she's
done...
Creon: Your happiness as well as mine, you fool.
Antigone: You disgust me, all of you, you and your happiness!'

                                      Anouilh p.47.

Antigone and Haemon are the youth caught in familial conflicts and can be understood as trampled humanity. In Anouilh's Antigone, the dialogue between Creon and Antigone is longer than its Sophocerian 'source text'. This accommodated contemporary French Existentialism which understood the world as absurd and the social agent is responsible for the consequences of their actions. Antigone embraced praxis. The 'love-interest' between the couple and Creon's familial compassion represented a different tone to Sophocles. Haemon mirrored *Camera obscura* Antigone:
Haemon - you can't let them take her away from me!
Here enjambment stresses the bourgeois individualism of 'me':
Creon: Yes, my boy – I can. Come now – courage.
The caesuras emphasis Creon self-belief, almost arrogance:

Haemon: It is over already.
Anouilh, p. 51

The Prophet[16] illustrates an example of the prophet as an intertextual motif. A powerful figure in some epochs and an outcast in others. The ruling classes were often too blinded by their power and wealth to hear the prophet's words. So, in Sophocles *Antigone* Creon had an almost paranoid belief that Teiresias was acting out of self-interest or money. The audience knew that Creon 's integrity had been compromised because of Athenian perspectives about the afterlife. Having entombed Antigone who belongs in a world of mortals and prevented the journey, by the necessary burial rites, of her brother, Polyneices, to Hades. Still, Creon believed the prophet spoke falsely:

Creon: Be sure you will not buy off my resolve.
Tiresias: Know that you will not live through many more races of the sun before you give one born of your loins as a corpse of exchange for corpses!
Sophocles, L 1030-33.

This scanned because the origins of poetry were in the chants of Shaman:

Poetry has grown out of magic.[17]

Contrasting with the prosaic prose line spoken by Creon who was damned by the gods. He too late sought refuge in the 'established laws' (Sophocles, L.1074). Creon sought a "synthesis"

---

[16] Isaac Deutscher *The Prophet: The Life of Leon Trotsky* (London, Verso Books, 2015).
[17] George Thompson, *Marxism and Poetry* (London. Lawrence & Wishart, 1946) p.13.

that did not exist, one which would not generate further dialectical conflicts and that the condemnation of Teiresias made quite apparent:

> Such arrows have I fired like an archer at your heart, in anger, for you have provoked me; arrows which are true, and you shall not escape their sting.'

Sophocles L. 1048-59

To remark on Antigone as a protagonist in Greek drama, where she would have been acted by a man in 5 B.C. with a mask, and whose 'voice' was silenced in the *performance text.* Sartre's position had cogency:
that the ancient playwright had a relationship with his audience it was simply impossible to replicate.[18]
Yet as an intertextual voice because she found resonance in literary characters like Vera Pavlova[19] or Nora[20]. They may not be 'sisters' of 'kin' but of 'struggle', forerunners of 'New Woman'. Dyadic opposites to Creon. I have attempted to shown how my initial method was embellished by Freudo-Marxist and Feminist literary analysis and that the dialectic between Antigone and Creon continued in texts and was interpreted by other

---

[18] Lorna Hardwick and Robert Fraser *Readings for Block 1* (Milton Keynes, The Open University, 2010), p.16.
[19] Nikolai Chernyshevsky, *What Is to Be Done?* (Ithaca & London, Connell University Press, 1989).
[20] Henrik Ibsen, *Four Major Plays: Doll's House; Ghosts; Hedda Gabler; and The Master Builder* (Oxford, Oxford World's Classics, 2008).

critics. Antigone can be 'read' as a secular revolutionary. One cannot forget she acted in 5.B.C. from conservative religious beliefs. The Cairo 2002[21] performance might have synthesised both political and religious aspects for the audience. MacNeice's second red dawn of civilisation remained a shimmer before tomorrow's morning.

---

[21] Timberlake Wertenbaker '*Antigone*', (Cairo production, directed by Frank Bradley, 2002.)

Bibliography.
Primary Texts.
Anouilh, J *Antigone* (trans Barbara Bray, London, Bloomsbury, 2013).
Aristotle, *Poetics* (trans Heath, M. London, Penguin Classics, 1996).
Sophocles, *Antigone*, (Cairo production, directed by Frank Bradley, 2002).
Sophocles, *Antigone* (trans David Franklin and John Harrison, Cambridge, Cambridge University Press, 2003).
Sophocles, *Antigone* (trans, Brown, A.L Oxford, Oxbow Books, 2014).
Sophocles, *The Three Theban Plays: 'Antigone', 'Oedipus the King', 'Oedipus at Colonus'* (trans, Robert Fagles, London, Penguin Classics, 1984).

Secondary Texts.
Badiou, A, *A Theory of the Subject* (London, Continuum, 2009).
Bernstein, J. M. *Hegel's Feminism* [Ed] Fanny Söderbäck Feminist Readings of Antigone (SUNY series in Gender Theory, State University of New York Press, 2010).
Blackledge, P, *Reflections on the Marxist theory of History* (Manchester, Manchester University Press, 2006).
Cairns, D, Sophocles: *Antigone* (Oxford, Bloomsbury, 2016).
Caudwell, C, *Illusion and Reality* (London, Lawrence & Wishart, 1946).
Chernyshevsky, N, *What Is to Be Done?* (Ithaca & London, Connell University Press.1989).
Clayton, J and Rothstein, E, 'Figures in the Corpus: Theories of Influence and Intertextuality',

Nigel Pearce Selected Work

in *Influence and Intertextuality in Literary History* (Madison, WI: The University of Wisconsin Press, 1991).

de Sousa Correa and Owens, W.R. *The Handbook of Literary Research*, (London, Routledge and The Open University, 2010).

Deutscher, I. *The Prophet: The Life of Leon Trotsky* (London, Verso Books, 2015).

Garvie, A, F. *The Plays of Sophocles* (London, Bloomsbury, 2016).

Jameson, F. *The Political Unconscious: Narrative as a socially symbolic act* (London, Routledge Classics, 2002).

Hardwick, L and Fraser, R. Readings *for Block 1* (Milton Keynes, The Open University, 2010).

Hardwick, L and Fraser R. *Reading Guide for Block 1: Antigone across* worlds (Milton Keynes, The Open University, 2010).

Harrison, T. *The Gaze of the Gorgon*. (Newcastle-upon-Tyne: Bloodaxe Books, 1992).

Ibsen, H. *Four Major Plays: Doll's House; Ghosts; Hedda Gabler; and The Master Builder*, (Oxford, Oxford World's Classic, 2008).

MacNeice, L, *Selected Literary Criticism* Ed. Alan Heuser (Oxford, Clarendon 1987).

Steiner, G, *The Antigone Myth in Western Literature, Art and, Thought* (Oxford, Oxford University Press, 2003).

Ormand, K, [ed] *A Companion to Sophocles* (Oxford, Wiley Blackwell, 2015).

Swift, L *Greek Tragedy; Themes and Contexts,* (London, Bloomsbury, 2016).

Thompson, G, *Marxism and Poetry* (London. Lawrence & Wishart, 1946).

Williams, R, *Marxism and Literature* (Oxford: Oxford University Press, 1994).
Žižek, S, *Antigone* (London: Bloomsbury, 2016).

The Evangelicals and Women in Community

How do differences in gender, class and age help define the nature of the Evangelical conversion experience and how far do some of the fictional characters of George Elliot and Hannah More illustrate the lived reality of the experience in late 18th and 19th century Britain?

Nigel Pearce

CONTENTS

Section Headings ....

    Primary Sources

    Secondary Sources

Aims of the Project and its Relationship to Course Issues
and the Secondary Sources ....

Conclusion ....

Bibliography ....

Nigel Pearce Selected Work

Aims of the Project and its Relationship to Course Issues and the Secondary Sources

This project attempts to create a coherent analysis of the relationship between elements such as gender, class and age in the context of the Evangelical conversion experience in late 18th and 19th century Britain. It will employ secondary sources, e.g. Luker, and the debate around Sunday Schools will be paramount. Fictional characters drawn from Hannah More and George Elliot[1] will embellish this project. Central to the question is the definition of Evangelicalism provided by Bebbington[2].

The paramount aim of the project is thematic in nature, i.e. the competing narratives such as gender, class and age creates a structure which is "relatively autonomous" in nature and in which we can examine and define conversionists experiences this structure is a complex model.

Firstly, this project will define a definition of conversionism[3]. This account of Evangelicalism, which provides a vivid account of the most extraordinary altered states of consciousness firstly in experience "wrestling with God" ("I saw Jesus hanging on the cross saying that your sins are forgiven") and finally "all guilt is gone and my soul was filled with unutterable peace"[4].

This delineation of a conversion experience contains a number of essential trends, the denial or wrestling with God, the direct and personal experience of

---

[1] Hannah More (1889), The History of Hester Wilmot, p123, George Elliot (1858), Scenes of Clerical Life, and George Elliot (1884), Adam Bede
[2] Bebbington, Evangelicalism in Modern Britain: A History from the 1730's to the 1980's, p5
[3] S Staniforth, Vol. 1 Wesley's Veterans, p5
[4] ibid, p5

crucicentrism and the purging of sins. "My soul was filled unutterable peace"[5]. This narrative of "agony and immense relief"[6] was archetypal in nature.

I am aware that preaching the gospel was a paramount method of converting individuals. The significance of conversionism was at its most salient when it was defined as marking the boundary between a "Christian and a pagan"[7]. However there was debate about the means of converting sinners Jonathan Edwards "believed in insisting on the reality of hell" (quoted in Bebbington)[8]. Methodism produced preachers who argued that "backsliders - the devil would soon toss them about in flames of hell with a pitchfork". The antithesis of Edwards was that "more emphasis should be laid on the forgiving love of God"[9]. So we have seen an essential conversion experience and it's consequences in creating cultural discourse and producing opposing tactics employed to convert, i.e. either hell or love. Intellectual debate with regard to the spiritual nature of conversionism was located within the Reformation. The Evangelicals argued against Catholicism and agreed with Luther that humanity is blemished by sin and that consequently even good works cannot be a path to salvation. It is only through justification by faith, i.e. by God's intervention rather than humanity's attempts at achieving salvation, that true redemption is achieved. However, within the Protestant tradition two models of conversionism are contested. Firstly there is the intense spiritual experience described by Stanford which is more proletarian in nature and secondly there is the

---

[5] Wesley's Veterans, p5
[6] Bebbington's Evangelicalism in Modern Britain: A History from the 1730's to the 1980's
[7] ibid, p5
[8] ibid, p5
[9] ibid, p6

gradualist approach of the Anglican Evangelicals. A leading theologian of this position stated "We require nothing sudden"[10].

As the 19th century developed, Evangelicalism became increasingly linked to bourgeois values. Examples of these developing links between Evangelicalism and bourgeois values can be seen by the growth of philanthropy and missionary work especially by middle class women. It is significant to perceive that the proletarian Early Methodism did not, in response, decline, but played an active role in dissent, e.g. Peterloo Massacre 1819. Finally, in this exploration of conversionism is a radical statement of a leading Baptist minister who in 1830 wrote "The sinner has powers to repent without the spirit"[11]. He later redefined his position. However nine students of Glasgow Congregational Theologists Academy were expelled in 1844 for self-conversionalism[12]. There would seem to have been a trend towards eliminated the elements of mystery from the conversion experience.

Differences in gender, class and age are all of significance in the process of defining and illuminating the complex nature of conversionism as can be seen from the secondary sources such as Halévy, Thompson, and Luker. This section is orientated to conversion experiences in the context of class. Halévy provides the foundation for assessing the social class nature of Evangelical conversionism.

He questions why wasn't there a revolution in 18th to 19th century England. He constructs a structure for this analysis and its elements, e.g. class, which is developed in the context of Methodism. Thompson develops and deepens Halévy's analysis.[13] Halévy's position is as follows "the elite of the working class in being

---

[10] Simeon on the New Birth
[11] Bebbington, Evangelicalism in Modern Britain: A History from the 1730's to the 1980's, p8
[12] ibid, p8
[13] Thompson, The Making of the English Working Class

viewed by Evangelical movement with the spirit for which the established order had nothing to fear"[14]. Hence class is essential to Evangelicalism. Conversionism was noted elsewhere because a converted worker would "work hard save money and assist his neighbour"[15]. Converted workers "solve the social problem"[16]. Sunday worship Thompson argued provided a sublimated sexual expression (Psychological Masturbation, Thompson) and it also provided the method of expressional repressed emotions[17]. These elements are paramount in understanding Evangelicalism as a process creating equilibrium under capitalism.

We have seen above and will see below the Thompson's model is contested, e.g. by Bebbington and Laqueur[18]. Thompson continues by addressing the pertinent questions put forward by Halévy. He argues that between the years 1790 to 1830 the direct indoctrination was of paramount significance especially with regard to Sunday Schools, with regard to proletarian experiences within Evangelicalism and to the centrality of conversionism. I will discuss first direct indoctrination, and second Methodist sense of community[19]. First the direct indoctrination can be examined in the context of Sunday Schools. An example of "religious terrorism" is apparent in Isaac Watts' "Divine Songs for Children" "There is not a sin that we commit nor wicked word we say that in thy dreadful book 'tis writ against the Judgement Day[20]. The abuse of children is apparent. It appears to be clear that Sunday School played a role in socialising children into passive and supine adulthood and that conversion experiences may, for example, emanate from a fear of God, as opposed to a love of

---

[14] Halévy 1906, The Birth of Methodism in England
[15] Bebbington Evangelicalism in Modern Britain: A History from the 1730's to the 1980's, p5
[16] N. G. During, Samuel Chadwick
[17] Quoted in Study Guide, p25
[18] Laqueur (1976), Religion and Respectability Sunday School and Working Class Culture
[19] ibid
[20] Watts, Diving Songs of Children, E. P. Thompson: The chiliasm of despair, off prints, p142 (A425)

viewed by Evangelical movement with the spirit for which the established order had nothing to fear"[14]. Hence class is essential to Evangelicalism. Conversionism was noted elsewhere because a converted worker would "work hard save money and assist his neighbour"[15]. Converted workers "solve the social problem"[16]. Sunday worship Thompson argued provided a sublimated sexual expression (Psychological Masturbation, Thompson) and it also provided the method of expressional repressed emotions[17]. These elements are paramount in understanding Evangelicalism as a process creating equilibrium under capitalism.

We have seen above and will see below the Thompson's model is contested, e.g. by Bebbington and Laqueur[18]. Thompson continues by addressing the pertinent questions put forward by Halévy. He argues that between the years 1790 to 1830 the direct indoctrination was of paramount significance especially with regard to Sunday Schools, with regard to proletarian experiences within Evangelicalism and to the centrality of conversionism. I will discuss first direct indoctrination, and second Methodist sense of community[19]. First the direct indoctrination can be examined in the context of Sunday Schools. An example of "religious terrorism" is apparent in Isaac Watts' "Divine Songs for Children" "There is not a sin that we commit nor wicked word we say that in thy dreadful book 'tis writ against the Judgement Day[20]. The abuse of children is apparent. It appears to be clear that Sunday School played a role in socialising children into passive and supine adulthood and that conversion experiences may, for example, emanate from a fear of God, as opposed to a love of

---

[14] Halévy 1906, The Birth of Methodism in England
[15] Bebbington Evangelicalism in Modern Britain: A History from the 1730's to the 1980's, p5
[16] N. G. During, Samuel Chadwick
[17] Quoted in Study Guide, p25
[18] Laqueur (1976), Religion and Respectability Sunday School and Working Class Culture
[19] ibid
[20] Watts, Diving Songs of Children, E. P. Thompson: The chiliasm of despair, off prints, p142 (A425)

God. Their spirituality may be debilitated for life. A competing analysis of the socio-cultural nature of the roles of Sunday Schools is provided by Laqueur[21]. He argues that Sunday Schools were institutions which employed mainly proletarian people and that they weaved a working class culture moulded by religion which was autonomous from the bourgeoisie, hence challenging the dominant ideology thesis. It is significant that over 2 million children[22] were sent to Sunday Schools. The question of Sunday Schools then centres on whether they were a) a place of religious terrorism or b) a relatively working class haven with inherently working class culture spirituality.

This dialectic is complex and multi-dimensional. It explores spirituality and the foundations of conversions in the context of fear of hell. However, what Evangelicalism can be seen by that class as inherent for independent working class socio-cultural refuge, and hence working class conversion experiences. Thompson also examines the Methodist community in relationship to the bourgeoisie and proletariat. Thompson argues that it is a community which was too euphoric[23]. But the open chapel doors "did offer to abandoned people the Industrial Revolution some kind of community."[24] Also Evangelicalism was not bound by the state and flourished in small discrete communities, e.g. tin mining[25], where "Revivalism in the limited localised sense of a sudden and spontaneous outburst of religious frenzy was experienced[26]. "These physical and psychic expressions, shrieks and the tear induced trances"[27] were examples of conversion experiences at their most florid. In

---

[21] Laqueur (1976),Religion and Respectability, Sunday School and Working Class Culture
[22] 1851 Religious Census quoted in A425 Study Guide, p75
[23] Thompson (1968), The Making of the English Working Class, p143
[24] ibid
[25] Luker (1980) Revivalism in theory and practice: The Case of Cornish Methodism
[26] ibid
[27] ibid

1851 "an estimated 43.8%" population of the country attended chapels on the day of the religious census[28]. Many experiences were condemned by the Weslyan authorities, who feared they evoked social discontent and popular protests. Hence we see the working class resistance ideology[29]. A minister, W J Warner, wrote that "as a result of great revivals in the past, the town, Penzance, swarms with backsliders, consequently popular revivalism could be the premise of a shallow and temporary conversion experience."[30] Hence there could be articulated a model "at times of depression the miners turn to riot rather than religion"[31] but may also experience hysterical conversion experiences and also at times of crisis seek solace in the chapel. Hence Luker illuminates a complex model connecting conversionism of class and chapel. He presents a tension between working class resistance ideology and which enabled it to support atrophied chapels based on volatile conversion experiences.

This theoretical case is examined as working class conversion experiences, e.g. by Thompson and Luker, we are left with a multi-dimensional model which ranges from "psychic masturbation", "religious terrorism", "the solace of the chapel", thus creating a positive conversionism and how conversion experiences could also be shallow.

This project is based on the following primary sources: George Elliot's, Scenes of Clerical Life and Adam Bede, and Hannah More's, The History of Hester Wilmot. These primary sources will be examined and then tested against the secondary sources discussed above. However, in order to ascertain what is necessary for historical enquiry the sources need to be examined in the context of

---

[28] ibid
[29] ibid
[30] Warner, The Wesleyan Movement in the Industrial Revolution, off prints, p35 (A425)

the writer's intellectual terrain. These themes, i.e. intellectual, spiritual and emotional, and the context of gender will define and illustrate Evangelical conversion experiences. This project will be primarily emanating from a gender perspective encapsulated as follows "the Victorian intense preoccupation with religious matters can only be compared to our own preoccupation with sexuality"[32]. Are these supposed opposites really "psychic masturbation"[33] in both 19th and 20th centuries. Here we can perceive the relationship between religion and sexuality, which feeds into conversion experiences.

A brief outline of Elliot's life will allow us to perceive her in the ethos in which she developed. The first for our purpose was her conversional experiences. However, as she read vociferously doubts began to erode her Evangelical faith in the Bible, divinely inspired became to Elliot a transition from faith to belief, i.e. she came to believe the Bible was a cultural item. She moved with her father to Coventry, and made the acquaintance of the local intellectuals[34]. They introduced her to Hennell's "An Inquiry into the Origins of Christianity". The Bible, Hennell argued was "essentially mythological writing"[35]. As a consequence of this process Elliot refrained from attending church. Elliot's intellectual development was rapid. The concept of realism addressed by Elliot is an attack on the "quality of romanticism" with its "rustic idles". "We have to be taught to feel or not be partisan of a sentimental peasant but for a peasant in all his coarse apathy and the artisan in all his suspicious selfishness"[36]. She also wrote "Art is the nearest thing to life, it is a

---

[31] Luker (1980), Revivalism in Theory and Practice: The Case of the Cornish Methodism
[32] David Lodge Introduction to 'Scenes from Clerical Life' p7
[33] Thompson (1968) The Making of the English Working Class
[34] Introduction from 'Scenes from Clerical Life', p13
[35] Hennell (1830) An Inquiry into the Origins of Christianity
[36] Essays of George Elliot (1968) ed. Pinney, Introduction, p15

mode of amplifying experiences extending our contact with our fellow men, beyond the bounds of our personal lot"[37]. Elliot's Scenes of Clerical Life replaces both Evangelicalism and false romanticism with realism which possessed both an aesthetic and a moral element. Elliot applies this realism to her characters and their introduction, e.g. the relationship of Janet Dempster and Mr Tryan is beyond caricature and moves beyond the "bounds of our personal life"[38]. Elliot delineates her method saying "I undertake to exhibit nothing as it should be; I only try to exhibit some things as they have been or are, seen through such a medium as my own nature gives me"[39], "A metaphorical vehicle of humanist values"[40].

We shall continue our examination of conversionism, firstly with middle class gender issues and their relationship to defining Evangelicalism. The project will draw themes from 'Janet's Repentance' in "Scenes of Clerical Life". Elliot has created a model of conversionism in Janet's Repentance. She is married to a drunken violent man. In order to cope with this benighted state she herself seeks solace in alcohol. However, Janet continues to carry out good works. We can perceive a middle class woman, while experiencing inner tempest, fulfilling her role as a philanthropist and the Evangelical preacher who ultimately becomes Janet's mentor and companion. Elliot is exhibiting the collision and the drama as not at all between bigoted churchmanship and Evangelicalism, but between irreligion and religion. Religion in this case happens to be represented by Evangelicalism[41]. For Elliot her "doctrine of sympathy" influenced by Feuerbach's 'The Essence of Christianity'[42] "Out of that heart out of the inward impulse to live and to die for man" creates a humanist model.

---

[37] Elliot (1848) Scenes from Clerical Life, p170-171
[38] ibid
[39] George Elliot letters
[40] Elliot, An introduction David Lodge, p8
[41] The George Elliot Letters ed. J S Haight, p347
[42] Feuerbach, The Essence of Christianity, Chapter 5, p3

So Janet's agony can be presented as a reaction to her husband's own poverty of the "original humanity"[43]. Hence we can understand religion being as a metaphor of humanism.

The process of Janet's conversion was articulated first from the ruin of alcohol and finally Janet's ejection from her own home. "Robert has turned me out. I have been in the cold a long while"[44]. She feels that she has no faith, no love left. The pivotal moment to Janet is when Mr Tryan "converts" by confiding his own sinful past. This expression of his hidden solidarity is clear with her. For Elliot Tryan's commitment to Evangelicalism is secondary to his humanity. Here we see our fellow men beyond the bounds of our own personal lot[45]. The metaphor for Elliot's scepticism to reconciliation in scenes with regard to her orientation to Christianity is "a sacred kiss" between hero and heroine, which concludes Scenes of Clerical Life. Hence religion is "perceived in a secular dimension".

This project will now examine Elliot's Adam Bede. It is a qualitatively different in that it is a story of working class characters, e.g. Dinah Morris, "they tell me is as poor as ever she was, works at a mill and "has much to do to keep herself"[46]. Her sermons can be contrasted with Mr Tryan's less ebullient expression. However, Dinah Morris also perceived a gentle cradling dimension of herself. She can be described in this statement "our moral progress may be measured by the degree in which we sympathise with individual suffering and individual joy"[47]. Also "sympathy", the one poor word which includes all our best insight and all our best love from pain

---

[43] Scenes from Clerical Life Introduction, David Lodge
[44] Scenes from Clerical Life, p340
[45] Essays of George Elliot ed. Pinney, p170-171
[46] Elliot, Adam Bede (1889), p63
[47] Elliott, Letter 15th November 1875

into sympathy[48]. Here Dinah is creating a religion of sympathetic humanity so 'Adam Bede' commences with a war taking place against the revolutionary French and Wordsworth and Colleridge's mould breaking lyrical ballads. This is the contrast which this project will address. Firstly, there is the contradictory nature of Dinah Morris. Two elements will be examined. Firstly her sermon addressed to Bessy Cranage who was wearing "large round earrings with false garnets in them"[49]. "Poor child he is beseeching you and you don't listen now he looks at you with love and mercy and says come to me that you may have life or depart from me into everlasting fire"[50]. Dinah continues her forceful speech to Bessy with regard to her earrings. "Ah, hear those follies, cast them away from you as if they were stinging adders. They are stinging you. They are poisoning your soul. They are dragging you into a dark bottomless pit where you will soon sink forever and forever before I go away from light and God"[51]. Dinah expresses her own self image "God has called me to minister to others and not have any joys or sorrows of my own but rejoice with them who are saved[52]". This position can be perceived as Evangelical activism. In contrast to her religious terrorism which is unleashed on Bessy Cranage is her treatment of Lizbeth Bede in mourning for her husband who drowned. Dinah travels to the Bede cottage to comfort Lizbeth in her mourning. This mourning was made manifest by "rocking herself, grasping the low moan with every forward movement of her body when she suddenly felt a hand placed gently on hers and a sweet voice said to her 'dear sister, the Lord has sent me to be a comfort to you'". Lizbeth achieves a degree of equilibrium from Dinah's soothing behaviour. Lizbeth responds

---

[48] Elliot, Adam Bede, p488
[49] ibid, p22
[50] ibid, p32
[51] ibid, p32
[52] ibid

"I wouldn't mind if you'd stay and sleep here" and to her magnanimity "fetch Adam's new Bible with pictures in and she shall read us a chapter, I like them words in the Bible". Dinah and Seth were both innately offering thanks for the greater quietness of spirit that had come down over Lizbeth. This is what Dinah had been trying to bring about though all her still sympathy and abstinence from exaltation[53].

A graphic contrast is apparent here from the agonies of hell to the soothing compassion of sacred secular love we are made aware of the complex nature of Evangelicalism and it can present itself as dialectical. There are contradictions within its totality thus the conflicting poles, i.e. fire and love achieves a need for a synthesis, a totality of Evangelicalism which can reconcile its opposites in a synthesis which can be understood to reside with Dinah. Hence the apparent paradox is resolved. Fire and love are reconciled in a working class woman preacher.

Now we shall examine the primary source, The History of Hester Wilmot[54]. This perspective will be contrasted with two secondary sources, i.e. Laqueur (1976) Religion and Respectability in Sunday Schools and Working Class Culture. More's tract can best be seen as an Evangelical didactic tract however, its lack of characterisation is stereotypically combined with a simplistic plot. Essentially it is propaganda directed at the proletariat. We will briefly delineate the development of the tract. Rebecca, Hester's mother had a violent, uncontrollable temper. She was fastidious with regard to domestic chores. Her behaviour was such that John, her husband, having no corner to run to, took to the ale house so that which was at first

---

[53] ibid, p114
[54] Hannah More (1834) The History of Hester Wilmot, p127

a refuge too soon became a pleasure. As the dark, dire domestic situation declined he became lost in self-indulgence. Mrs Jones opened a Sunday School. Perceiving that none of the Wilmots attended she visited. Mrs Jones maintained that she would "teach her to fear God". Rebecca's reply was "I would rather you would teach her to fear me and to keep my house clean". Hester Wilmot attended Sunday School regularly. Her desire for learning, was such that she would work early and late to give her a little time to read her Bible. A reading of the Bible and Catechism were the source of comfort for her. Hester, as a consequence of her reading, became aware of her sins. "We are by nature born to sin". But she soon found the spiritual grace by which we have a new birth and gained righteousness[55]. We have comprehended the spiritual metamorphosis of Hester Wilmot.

Now I am going on to the ideological role of Sunday Schools. "When children are bad, comfort yourself with thinking how much worse they would have been but for you and indeed what a burden they would come to society". This is an example of Sunday School as a dominant ideology thesis. However it is abundantly clear that some would seek solace in the working class culture. Again we are presented with the contradiction but unlike the dialectic described above, this cannot be resolved.

The dramatic conversion of Mr and Mrs Wilmot can be summarised here. Hester's religion caused conflict between Hester and her mother. Mrs Wilmot developed a dangerous fever, Hester denied herself and nursed her mother. When John by gambling, lost borrowed money from Hester, which she had saved for her gown, he "stammered out a broken excuse he had lost the money". Hester forgives her father and John walked away mournfully and said to himself surely there must be something in religion since it exhibits a change of heart. He pondered the change in

---

[55] Hannah More, The History of Hester Wilmot, p123

Hester from a pert girl to as mild as a lamb, from vain girl to one contented with rags. When after a family tempest, John hears Hester pray for her parents, he fell down on his knees, embraced his child and begged her to teach him how to pray. Rebecca also experienced a conversion. "She knelt down by her husband and joined in prayer with much fervour". It is self apparent that More's work is mundane and banal and is composed as an instrument of propaganda. The difference in age between Hester and self evidently her parents can be perceived as significant to Evangelical conversion and how it can be defined. Age and Evangelical conversion is of interest here.

This thesis will now examine three moments in Hetty's life, in Adam Bede. Firstly, "Hetty's dreams of all of luxuries, to sit on a path in pallor, to have some large beautiful earrings such as they were all the fashion"[56]. Hetty is perceived as superficial and her dreams were not of meanings beyond her desire for trinkets. Her emotional life after reading Arthur Donnithorne's letter were shallow "all the girlish passion and vanity that made up her love"[57]. So here we conclude the first episode of Hetty's journey. The second episode is structured around Arthur Donnithorne's seduction of Hetty, his departure from military duty and Hetty's pregnancy, hoping as promised that Arthur would help her. In distress she begins her journey in search of him. "Poor wandering Hetty, with the roundish childish face and the hard unloving despairing soul looking out of it"[58]. The narrator considers "what will be the end, the end of this objectless wandering clinging to life only as a wounded brute clings to it"[59]. Elliot is creating another dimension here for, as a parallel to Hetty's wanderings

---

[56] Elliot, Adam Bede (1859), p100
[57] Ibid, p335
[58] Ibid, p391
[59] Ibid, p391

in the objective material world, is another journey, a journey through her psyche, sometimes conscious sometimes unconscious. This is an interaction between her physical wandering which is pitiful and her dark abyss, this is a metaphor of archetypal magnitude. Hetty is arrested and found guilty of infanticide. Dinah enters the condemned cell. We are again presented with a metaphor of light and dark, day and night. Dinah holds Hetty "It was the human contact she'd come to but she was non the less sinking into the dark self. Dinah entreats Hetty to believe in a loving God who will forgive. If God our Father was your friend, was willing to save you from sin and suffering so as you would neither know wicked feelings nor pain again"[60]. Hetty does not respond and Dinah continues to encourage Hetty to "open your heart". There is a cordial relationship between Hetty's desire for secular comfort. "You won't leave me Dinah will you? You'll hang close to me". And Dinah's desire for spiritual salvation, Dinah perseveres. Dinah persuades Hetty to kneel "Dinah help me I can't feel anything like you, my heart is too hard."[61] Hetty confesses her crime to Dinah. Hetty clings round Dinah and shudders again. Elliot is ambiguous with regard to Hetty's conversion"[62]. What is apparent is that she experiences a cathartic experience and purgation. An experience of Hetty's conversion is not clear. It is possible to comprehend the dialogue in the condemned cell.

"One of human ruin, human love and the absolving process of two women sharing in the context of conversion, but the female caring defined as Evangelicalism as socio culture discourse provided a sense of emotional release. This can be illustrated in Elliot's 'Model of Secular Sympathy'. Nevertheless it is possible to perceive Hetty's experiences as spiritual for when Adam visited the condemned cell,

---

[60] ibid, 450
[61] ibid, p451
[62] ibid, p455

Nigel Pearce

This analysis will construct an overview in order to provide a detailed analysis of socio economic class and social cultural matters within the context of the Evangelical conversion experience. It will become apparent that, not only did the Proletariat not attend church en masse, but the different strata of the working classes attended in different numbers, e.g. artisan made up to 23% of society, but 59% of Evangelicals non conformity. Unskilled workers made up an even smaller number of chapel attenders. Early Methodists in Lincolnshire 51% of lay preachers were agricultural labourers[65]. Developing this theme early Methodists, in the first part of the 19th century were composed as follows: 15% labourers, 20% miners, 43% artisans[66].

Here we come to perceive a connection with Halévy analysis "the elite of the working class is being embued by Evangelical movements with the spirit which in established order have nothing to fear"[67]. Hence it is apparent that the majority of the proletarians did not attend church "for adherence"[68]. Seth Bede is an example illuminating Halévy's thesis since, as an artisan and a Methodist he appears to be totally unaware of the class struggle that his class strata would lead, with a defeat to any particular unrest, e.g. the United Irish Rebellion (1789) led by Wolf Tone, who was a Protestant. A pattern can be perceived here when a political movement is perceived to be defeated "hope for improved conditions and political improvements in the present life". People responded by pinning their hopes or fears on the life to come. Thompson argued for an "Oscillation between political and religious excitement"[69]. As the latter increases the former subsided[70]. Mannheim articulates

---

[65] Obelkevich (1971) Religion and Rural Society: South Lindor 1825 - 1875
[66] Gilbert, Religion in Society, p63
[67] Halévy (1906) The Birth of Methodism in England
[68] Elliot (1854) Adam Bede
[69] Thompson, The Making of the English Working Class
[70] Study Guide p90

Nigel Pearce Selected Work

The theory of chiliasm "Chiliasm has always accompanied revolutionary outbursts and will give them rare spirit. When this spirit ebbs and deserts these movements, there remains behind in the world a naked mass frenzy and a dis-spiritualised fury"[71]. An example of chiliasm was the preaching of Joanna Southcott which flourished in the wake of the failure of British Jacobins and therefore the process of oscillation has swung from political to religion.

The rapid growth of Methodism during the wars was a component of the psychic process of counter revolution[72]. An example of this oscillation calls religion the hysterical conversion accompanying experiences is described by "a preacher of the Bible Christians". The conversion experiences were often accompanied by agonies, prostratorising and loud and pitying cries of penitence[73].

Socio-economic class and Methodism are symbiotic in nature. The most significant example of "spiritualised fury" were to be located in the movements which surround the major 'prophetess' Joanna Southcott. She preached her apocalyptic message to the masses "the lower class began to believe the seven seals are about to be opened[74]. Her apocalyptic fervour was closely akin to the fervours of early Methodism. It brought people to the point of hysterical intensity, the desire for personal salvation was intense. Again we can perceive a causal relationship between socio economic class and conversion experiences. The nature of the conversion experiences in the 18th and 19th centuries above is proletarian and we should expect this as a component element of the chiliasm of despair.

---

[71] Manheim (1960) Ideology and Utopia
[72] Thompson (1968) The Making of the English Working Class
[73] F W Bourge (1905) The Bible Christians
[74] Southey (1908) Letters from England

Having explored the working class, and their conversion experiences, this project will now examine middle class responses to conversionism and its consequence. An example from Scenes from Clerical Life (Elliot, 1858) is of interest. We shall explore Miss Rebecca Linnet. She possessed a sense of fashion which was transformed by the heroine of the novel which she was engaged with. However, "No-one could deny that Evangelism had brought a change for the better in Rebecca Linnet's person"[75]. A plain grey denim dress and plain white collar could never have belonged to her before that date. This is a change in her and expression which seems to shed a softened light over her person. Mr Tryan is not extreme but a "softened life". Rebecca Linnet, like many Methodist converts, was strengthened by the doctrine of assurance, and became involved in philanthropic work. Gender roles were addressed by Evangelicalism but as the 19th century progressed there was a decline in working class with preaches, e.g. Dinah Morris, and the rise in middle class philanthropy, e.g. Rebecca Linnet.

This project will now illustrate the question of age. The phrase "religious terrorism", is employed to illuminate the treatment of some children in Sunday School. The Commission on Mines interviewed a ten year old girl "If I died a good girl I would go to heaven and if I were bad I should have burned in brimstone and fire. They told me that at Sunday School and I did not know it before"[76]. This is an example of the relationship between age and Evangelicalism.

Another point about the relationship between age and Evangelicalism is that conversion was most common amongst teenagers[77]. Connected to this general observation is "the mean age of conversion among future Methodist ministers in the

---

[75] Elliot (1858) Scenes from Clerical Life, p268
[76] Cited in J L Hammond, Lord Shaftesbury, Quoted in A425 off prints, p142
[77] Bebbington, Evangelicalism in Modern Britain: A History from the 1730's to 1980's, p7

period 1780 to 1890 was 16.4 years. The mean age in the period 1841 to 1900 was 15.8[78]. An example of teenage conversion is delineated in the History of Hester More. She was 14 years old when she converted at Sunday School and succeeds in converting her parents so we have a spectrum of age from 10 years old to 16 years old. There is also the range of experience in Methodist ministers conversion in mid teens to the brutal indoctrination of a 10 year old girl at Sunday School. Although Hannah More can be perceived as propaganda, she carefully places Hester at the most fertile age for conversion, 14. Teenage conversions can be explained by youthful idealism and following Thompson, an awakening in sexuality which was sublimated.

Briefly we will glance at assurance. Its roots lie in the conversion experience that normally accompany it. The foundation "has its roots in the inward persuasion that God was on their side"[79]. The doctrine of assurance provided a foundation of Evangelicalism.

Conclusion

Differences in gender, class and age helps define Evangelical conversion experiences. Firstly, we examined gender and class. The working class preacher Dinah can be seen as preaching the hell method of encouraging conversionism. But she also exhibits great compassion in nursing of Lizbeth Bede. She is in the tradition of the early Methodism and expressions of conversionism were intense and exhibited a more sublimated sexuality[80]. Elizabeth Linnet, who is a product of the developing gradualist tradition throughout the 19th century, provides an alternative "soft light". This is in stark contrast to the early Methodism. Mr Tryan is also in the

---

[78] ibid, p7
[79] Bebbington, Evangelicalism in Modern Britain: A History from the 1730's to the 1980's, p7

context, in that he expresses middle class gradualism, a stark contrast to the conversion experiences of Dinah Morris. We can perceive the demise of early Methodism and the rise of Anglican Evangelicalism during the 19th century. Middle class women became involved in philanthropic enterprises, e.g. Josephine Booth.

The question of age was addressed in relation to Evangelical experiences which were mainly teenage. This can be explained by youthful idealism and an emerging sexuality[81]. Conversion experiences have socio cultural expressions which can be perceived as a "chiliasm of despair" with a religious response to political defeat in terms of popular support, e.g. for Joanna Southcott. Therefore we can perceive those conversion experiences in the context of the defeats of the class struggle. However the method developed above suggests a complex socio cultural model which led to workers resistance ideology and the solace of the chapel.

---

[80] Thompson (1968) The Making of the English Working Class
[81] ibid

Nigel Pearce Selected Work

Bibliography

Primary Sources

A425 Study Guide

Elliot (1858), Scenes from Clerical Life

Elliot (1859), Adam Bede

Elliot, (1968) Essays of George Elliot, Ed. Pinney

Elliot, The George Elliot Letters

Hennell (1830), An Enquiry into the Origins of Christianity

Feuerbach (1844), The Essence of Christianity

More, Hannah, The History of Hester Wilmot

Southey, Letters from England

Watts, Divine Songs for Children

Secondary Sources

Bebbington, Evangelism in Modern Britain: A History from the 1730's to the 1980's

Bourge (1905), The Bible Christians

Bocock & Thompson, Religion and Ideology

During, Samuel Chadwick

Hammond, G. L. & Hammond, B., Lord Shaftesbury

Halévy (1906), The Birth of Methodism in England

Laqueur (1976), Religion and Respectability and Working Class Culture

Luker, Revivalism in Theory and Practice: The Case of Cornish Methodism in A425 Off Prints Collection

Mannheim (1960), Ideology and Utopia

Marx, Thesis on Feuerbach

Obelkevich (1971), Religion and Rural Society: South Lindor

Simeon, Quote "On the New Birth"

Smart, The Religious Experience of Mankind

Stanford, Wesley's Veterans

Thompson (1968), The Making of the English Working Class in A425 Off Prints Collection

Warner, The Wesleyan Movement in the Industrial Revolution

Nigel Pearce

Jane Eyre and Christianity: an analysis.

This response to how differing schools of Christianity are personified in Helen Burns, Mr Brocklehurst and St John Rivers must necessarily recognise that the 1840s were one of intense contestation by 'organic intellectuals'. My analysis is positioned by the scholarship of Raymond Williams[22], Mikhail Bakhtin[23], Marx & Engels[24], New Historicists Heather Glen[25] and Marianne Thormählen[26] as well as postcolonialist theorists Edward Said[27] and Gayatri Spivak[28]. I shall argue, following Raymond Williams, that the industrial revolution was the determinant for the Victorian novel. Although Raymond Williams argued that *Jane Eyre* and *Wuthering Heights* are very different from Charles Dickens' novels they represented a similar "clashing' with the 'emergent system". For Williams, the basis of the novel in

---

[22] Raymond Williams, *The Novel from Dickens to Lawrence* (London: Chatto & Windus 1984).
[23] Mikhail Bakhtin *The* Dialogic *imagination: Four Essays* (Austin, University of Texas Press 2014)
[24] Marx Engels *On Religion (Moscow, Progress Publishers* 1975)
[25] Heather Glen, *Charlotte Bronte: The Imagination in history ((Oxford: Oxford University Press.* 2002).
[26] Marianne Thormählen, *The Bronte's and Religion* (Cambridge: Cambridge University Press, 1999).
[27] Edward Said, Culture and Imperialism (London: Vintage Book 1994)
[28] Gayatri Spivak Three women texts: a critique of imperialism. (1985).

this period was that of 'the crisis of the knowable community'. Williams defined this community as one in which 'known relationships about a whole social structure... in which persons themselves can be wholly known' [29] they were disintegrating. Brontes novels:

> Belongs I think, in the moving earth... The world we need to remember if we are to connect with the 1840s is the world of Blake: a world of hunger, of rebellion and of pallid convention.[30]

Delia da Sousa Correa[31] suggested a reading informed by Mikhail Bakhtin, a Russian Formalist. I found Bakhtin provided significant insights into literary theory. He had argued Bennett[32] answered the autonomous system of 'signs', 'signifiers' and 'signified' delineated by Saussure[33] in his model of *langue* and *parole*. This was because for Russian Formalists the problem was in essence 'literariness', it was synchronic as it was for Saussure. For Bakhtin, the text was almost lifted out of History, but not to the same degree as Saussure in that social setting was significant. Bakhtin argued Tolstoy had provided a monologic

---

[29] Raymond Williams pp 16-17
[30] ibid, p, 60.
[31] Delia Da Sousa Correa *The Nineteenth Century Novel: Realisms* (Milton Keynes, Open University 2004) p. 106.
[32] Tony Bennett, *Formalism and Marxism*, (London: Methuen & Co) p, 51-2.
[33] Saussure, *Course in General Linguistics*, (Chicago, Open Court, 1998).

reading of the genre while Dostoevsky offered a dialogic or 'multi-voiced reading.' I argue that Charlotte Bronte also achieved this using *'Hetroglossia'* in *Jane Eyre* and with a fusion of religious alienation as described by the young Marx and commodity fetishism as delineated by the mature Marx I attempt to provide an explanatory model for the exploration of 1) Christianity as portrayed in three major characters, 2) the related 'many-voiced' nature of *Jane Eyre*. Thus, in making my argument I intent to employ both 'Historicist' and 'Formalist' methodologies.

When a reader is engaged with any text, they must have ascertained its genre to comprehend it. The genre of the bourgeois and early capitalism was the novel. Ian Watt[34] argued the Realist novel arose out of Protestant individualism as Jane said:

I care for myself. The more solitary, the more friendless
I am…the more I respect myself. I will keep the law given
by God; sanctioned by man.[35]

It was possible to have perceived this genre is creating, in its early phases, a spiritualized individual based on the petty-bourgeoisie as in Defoe[36] that was later generalised into the

---

[34] Ian Watt, *The Rise of the Novel*, (London: Bodley Head 2015).
[35] Charlotte Bronte, *Jane Eyre*, 2008, (Oxford, Oxford University Press) p.317. Hereafter J.E p, #.
[36] Danial Defoe, *Robinson Crusoe*, (Oxford, Oxford University Press, 2008.)

bourgeoisie. A popular form of the novel became the 'Governess novel' with Jane Austin *Emma* (1816). Bronte made clear her opinion of Austin in this letter to G. H. Lewes:
Now I can understand admiration of George Sand…which if I cannot fully comprehend…she is sagacious and profound.
Miss Austin is only shrewd and observant.[37]

Jane Eyre disrupted the discourse of the 'governess novel' by using several genres e.g. Gothic. Another 'governess novel' was written by Calvinist Mary Jane Sherwood whose protagonist claimed to have found salvation through no deeds of her own but:

Through the merits and death of my Divine Redeemer.[38]
This variant on Protestantism which, being biblical literalist, believed an 'elect' was chosen at the beginning of Time, would be called by God on earth and eventually lead into Paradise. Charlotte Bronte *Jane Eyre* was more complex and not a simple reflex of a single voice or genre.
Conventionality is not morality. Self-righteousness is not
religion. To attack the first is not to assail the last. To pluck
the mask from the face of the Pharisee, is not to lift

---

[37] Charlotte Bronte *Letters* [Ed] *Margret* Smith (Oxford, Oxford University Press, 2007), p.99.
[38] *Mary Jane Sherwood, Caroline Mordaunt, or The Governess* (1835).

an impious hand to the Crown of Thorns.

J.E, p. 4,

An important feature in the governess novel genre is that most novels depicted progress towards maturity or improvement for the heroine. It should be noted that her development is not stereotypically 'feminine'; like the male hero of the Bildungsroman, she leaves her home and goes out into the world alone. Although the governess lived and worked within a domestic sphere, but was still living with strangers. The governess-novel, Delia da Sousa Correa, argued 'was an extremely popular kind of fiction'[39] which could be defined as either 'providential' or 'romantic'[40] 'written by female authors for largely female readers.'[41] The former mode concluded with a spiritual realisation and the latter with marriage to the employer. So, whether the woman protagonist was a 'fallen petty-bourgeois woman' or an 'orphan' the governess novel would provide a socially acceptable denouncement for what was a tangible problem in early/mid-Victorian society i.e. impoverishment of unmarried middle-class women and orphans. However, it is noteworthy that Florence Nightingale thought orphan-hood necessary in women's literature to provide the freedom required to have achieved any degree of independence. She suggested:

---

[39] Delia Da Sousa Correa pp. 98-100.
[40] ibid p.99.
[41] ibid.

The heroine generally has no family ties (almost *invariably* no mother), or, if she does, these do not interfere with her entire independence.[42]

Marx critiqued Ludwig Feuerbach[43] who was translated into English by George Eliot. Feuerbach argued that humanity 'projected' its essence into the clouds and called it Divinity, humans, therefore, reified and/or personified their essence. Feuerbach had drawn philosophical conclusions based on Higher Criticism of the Bible which was focused on literary analysis and historical research. Lower Criticism attempted to establish an original and correct reading of the Bible. The young Marx wanted to understand why people would want to estrange themselves; he begun to write in 1843-4. He argued that. Feuerbach had a foundation in socio-economic life:
Religious suffering is... the expression of real suffering and a protest at real suffering. Religion is the sigh of the oppressed
creature the heart of a heartless world, and the soul of soulless   conditions.
It is the opium of the people. The abolition of religion as the illusory happiness of the people is the demand for their real happiness...
It is to call on them to give up a condition that requires illusions. The criticism of religion is,

---

[42] Patsy Stoneman *Charlotte Bronte*, Writers and their Work, (Northcote: British Council, 2013). p. 34.
[43] Ludwig Feuerbach, *The Essence of Christianity*, (New York: Prometheus Books,1989)

therefore, in embryo, the criticism of that vale of tears of which religion is the halo.
Criticism has plucked the imaginary flowers on the chain not in order that man shall continue to bear that chain without fantasy or consolation, but so that he shall throw off the chain and pluck the living flower. [44]

It seemed that Bronte employed twin phallic stone metaphors to describe the two male Evangelicals. Firstly, Mr Brocklehurst:

A black pillar! — such, at least, appeared to me, at first sight, the straight, narrow, sable-clad shape standing erect on the rug; the grim face at the top was like a carved mask.
J.E, p. 31.

Like all Christians, he believed humanity was tainted by Original Sin. He believed his calling was 'to correct Nature' as attempted in this exchange with Jane:

Do you know where the wicked go after death?
They go to hell was my ready and orthodox answer.
...
What must you do to avoid it?
I deliberated a moment; my answer...
I must keep in good health and not die.

J.E. p. 42

---

[44] Karl Marx, *Early Writing, (London: Penguin Marx Library, 1977)* p.244.

Secondly, the reader was shown the other side of the Calvinist/evangelical coin, St John Rivers who was a minister on the evangelical wing of the Anglican church. As Phrenology played an important role in Bronte's' worldview he was initially described:

A straight, classic nose; quite an Athenian mouth and chin.

J.E, p.345.

The mistake of judging a person by their appearances became apparent as his emotional ossification was revealed by metaphor:

He was no longer flesh, but marble: his eye was a cold, bright, blue, green gem, his tongue, a speaking instrument nothing more.

J.E, p. 411.

Terry Eagleton made an analogy between William Crimsworth in Bronte's *The Professor* and Rivers: Rivers is a spirited bourgeois eager to reap inexhaustible profits, unflaggingly devoted to the purchase of souls… an analogy between entrepreneur and evangelist.[45]

Rivers, in his fashion, is as offensive as Mr Brocklehurst, arrogant and conceited:

---

[45] Terry Eagleton Myths of Power: A Marxist Study of the Brontes (Cambridge: Cambridge University Press, 2005).

"My vocation? My great work? ... My hopes of being numbered in the band who have merged all ambitions in the glorious one
of bettering their race of carrying knowledge into the realms of ignorance…
J.E, p. 376.

Those two men were embodiments of elements [Hell] fire and water, 'ice.' In contrast, we read Helen Burns as the most informed of the Christians, one who believed in The Doctrine of Universal Salvation:

A new commandment I give unto you, that ye love one another; as I have loved you,
—John 13:34-35 (KJV).
Helen to Jane:

It is not violence that best overcame – nor vengeance that most certainly heals injury
J.E, p. 58.

New Historicist studies by firstly, Heather Glen[46] maintained that once Elizabeth Gaskell (1857) biography of Charlotte Bronte illuminated the fact that Loward School run by Mr Brocklehurst was a fictionalised version of the Clergy Daughters School at Cowan Bridge where the Bronte sisters Maria and Elizabeth died of tuberculosis. Brocklehurst being a characterization of the headmaster there, Rev. Carus Wilson. Maria the model for Helen. A loved and deceased sibling

---

[46] Glen, 2002

might have been rather overly idealised as Helen Burns.

In her depiction of the horrors of Jane's childhood Charlotte Bronte is responsible for a major social and historical fact of early ninetieth century England.[47]

However, Marianne Thormählen tends to differ from Glen:

The Bronte fiction reflects a reliance on Divine forgiveness which transcends the views that prevailed in the authors' time.[48]

I note Gayatri Spivak maintained:

It should not be possible to read nineteenth-century British literature without remembering that imperialism, understood as Britain's social mission, was a crucial representation of England to the English.[49]

She understood Jane Eyre's "self-marginalized uniqueness" as a "family/counter family dyad" around which Bronte's novel is structured and argued that this was achieved through imperialist ideology and constructed using dyads: human/animal, madness/reason, England/not-England. Ultimately Jane must remove Rochester's mad, Creole wife Bertha Mason to

---

[47] ibid. p.68.
[48] Marianne Thormählen, (1999), p.219.
[49] Gayathri Spivak, (1985) p, 243.

take her place in the family. What cannot be resisted is that Bertha must die for the novel to 'work'. Bronte's description of Bertha is deeply troubling from both a post-colonialist and a 'disability' perspective:

> What it was, whether beast or human being, one could not, at first sight tell: it grovelled, seemingly, on all fours; it snatched and growled like some strange wild animal: but it was covered with clothing, and a quantity of dark, grizzled hair, wild as a mane, hid its head and face.
>
> J.E. p. 257.

I also maintain that although Jane is a first-person narrator she is fragmented because she speaks with several 'voices': the passionate and rebellious child who meets Helen Burns and punished by Mr Brocklehurst, the adolescent who meets Miss Temple, the young governess who falls in love with Rochester but will not live outside of marriage with him, a runaway who finds solace at Moor House and although willing to accompany St. John Rivers in his missionary work refuses to marry for ideological reasons and finally her conversion of the now maimed Byronic Rochester to prayer. Does the reader ever know Jane? Does she travel between ideologues assuming different persona? She had become almost a 'commodity'. Edward Said[50] described in his analysis of Austin *Mansfield Park,* and Spivak[51] makes clear both

---

[50] Edward Said, (1994). pp, 69-70, 100-116.
[51] Gayathri Spivak, (1985).

Jane and Rochester were living off the ill-gotten fruits of imperialism, the lower depths of capital accumulation, human slavery. Not what I would call Christian values because Britain used slavery in its phase of 'primitive accumulation':

The beginning of the conquest and looting of the East Indies, the turning of Africa to a warren for the commercial hunting of black-skins.... These idyllic proceedings are the chief moments of primitive accumulation. [52]

Marx cogently linked religious alienation with commodity fetishism:

The commodity-form... It is nothing but the definite social relation between men themselves which assumes here, for them, the fantastic form of a relation between things. *In* order therefore, to find an analogy we must take flight into the misty realm of religion. There the products of the human brain appear as autonomous figures endowed with a life of their own, which enter into relations both with each other and with the human race. So, it is in the world of commodities with the products of men's hands.
I call this the fetishism which attaches itself to the products of labour as soon as they are produced as commodities[53]

---

[52] Karl Marx, Capital, *(London: Penguin Classics)* vol 1 Ch 31.
[53] Karl Marx (1990) p. *165*.

This I suggest lay at the heart of the alienated world in which the characters lived. It was, therefore, consistent that the novel concluded with the final quote from the fantastical Book of Revelations, the last book of the Bible. Written in approximately AD 90 to rally the Church as it faced disappointment because the eschatological prophecies of the Gospels were not realised. The first book of the New Testament to be written was 'Acts of the Apostles' in around AD 40 and had illustrated the early church expected the promised Messiah imminently:

The last letter I received from him drew from my eyes human tears, and yet filled my heart with Divine joy . . . no fear of death will darken St. John's last hour: his mind will be
unclouded; his heart will be undaunted; his hope will be sure; his faith steadfast. His own words are a pledge of this:
"My Master," he says, "has forewarned me. Daily he announces more distinctly, 'Surely I come quickly;" and hourly I more eagerly respond, — 'Amen; even so come,
Lord Jesus!'"

J.E.

p.556.

The 'problem ending' is explained by materialist analysis of a dialogic novel. I, however, speculate that Helen Burns' voice was lost in a Calvinist gale across the Yorkshire moors. The novel's Christianity could be contrasted with the visionary Socialism depicted in William Morris (1890) *News from Nowhere*[54]. Both may be envisaged as solutions to Raymond William's 'crisis of the knowable community'.

---
[54]

[https://www.marxists.org/archive/morris/works/1890/nowhere/nowhere.htm]

Bibliography.
Primary Sources.

Austin, J, *Emma*, (London: Wordsworth Editions, 2000).

Austin, J, *Mansfield Park* (London: Penguin Classics,1996).

Bible, King James Version (New York: HarperCollins, 2011).

Bronte, C, *Jane Eyre*, [ed] Richard J. Dunn, (London: Norton Critical Edition, 2001).

Bronte, C, *Jane Eyre*, [ed] Q. D. Leavis, (Harmondsworth: The Penguin English Library, 1968).

Bronte, C, Jane *Eyre*, [ed] Margaret Smith, (Oxford: Oxford University Press, 2008).

Bronte, C, The *Poems of Charlotte Bronte*, [ed]Tom Winnifrith (Oxford: The Shakespeare Head Press 1984).

Bronte, C, S*elected Letters* [Ed] Margaret Smith, (Oxford: Oxford University Press, 2010).

Defoe, D, *Robinson Crusoe*, (Oxford: Oxford University Press, 2008)

Feuerbach, L, *The Essence of Christianity*. [trans, George Eliot] (New York: Prometheus Books, 1989).

Marx, K, *Capital.* (London: Penguin Classics, 1990).

Marx, K, Early *Writing,* (London: Penguin Marx Library, 1977).

Marx & Engels, *On Religion* (Moscow: Progress Publishers, 1975).

Morris, W: [https://www.marxists.org/archive/morris/works/1890/nowhere/nowhere.htm]

Sherwood, Mary Jane, *Caroline Mordaunt, or The Governess.* (Holborn Hill: William Darton and Son, 1985).

Secondary Sources.

Ashcroft, B, Griffins, G, Triffins, H, *Postcolonial Studies: The Key Concepts*, (London: Routledge, 2013).

Alexandra, C, Smith M, *The Oxford Companion to The Brontes,* (Oxford, Oxford University Press, 2012).

Bakhtin, M, *The Dialogic imagination: Four Essays*, (Austin, University of Texas Press, 2014).

Beaty, J, *Misreading Jane Eyre, A Postformalist Paradigm.* (Ohio: Ohio State University Press, 1996).

Bennet, T, *Formalism and Marxism*, (London: Methuen & Co, 1979).

Chadwick, O, *The Victorian Church Part One 1829-1859* (London: SCM Press, 1971).

Da Sousa Correa, D, *The Twentieth Century Novel: Realisms*. (London& Milton Keynes: Routledge/Open University, 2004).

Da Sousa Correa, D, *Reading guide for Block 2 Jane Eyre* (Milton Keynes, The Open University, 2009).

Da Sousa Correa, D, *The Handbook of Literary Research* (London & Milton Keynes: Routledge & The Open University, 2010).

Eagleton, T, *Myths of Power: A Marxist Study of the Brontes* (London: Palgrave Macmillan). (Cambridge: Cambridge University Press, 2005).

Eagleton, T, *The English Novel: An Introduction*, (Oxford: Blackwell, 2005).

Gilbert M, Sandra & Gubar, Susan, The *Madwoman in the Attic: The Woman Writer and the Ninetieth Century Literary Imagination*. (New York: Yale University Press, 2000).

Glen, H (2002*) The Cambridge Companion to the Brontes,* (Cambridge: Cambridge University Press, 2002).

Nigel Pearce Selected Work

Glen, H, *Charlotte Bronte: The Imagination in history* (Oxford: Oxford Press).

Harman, C, *Charlotte Bronte: A Life* (London: Penguin Books 2016).

Holne, A & Wussow, H [eds], *A Dialogue of Voices: Feminist Literary Theory and Bakhtin.* (Minneapolis; University of Minneapolis Press, 1998).

Hultquist, M, *Dialogism, Bakhtin ad his World*, (London: Routledge 2002).

Ingram, P, *The Brontes, Authors in Context,* (Oxford: Oxford University Press, 2008).

Lodge, S, *Charlotte Bronte Jane Eyre: A reader's guide to essential criticism.* (New York: Palgrave Macmillan, 2009).

MacKay, M, *The Cambridge Introduction to The Novel,* (Cambridge: Cambridge University Press, 2011).

MacLeod, J, *Beginning Postcolonialism* (Manchester: Manchester University Press, 2010).

Mandel, E, *Marxist Economic Theory*, (London: Merlin Press, 1977).

Michie B, Elise [ed], *Charlotte Bronte's Jane Eyre: A Casebook,* (Oxford: Oxford University Press, 2006).

Rhys, J, *Wide Sargasso Sea*, (London: Penguin Modern Classics, 2000).

Said, Edward. W, *Culture and Imperialism*, (London: Vintage Books, 1994).

Saussure, *Course in General Linguistics*, (Chicago, Open Court, 1998).

Gayatri Spivak Three women texts: a critique of imperialism *Critical Inquiry, Vol. 12, No. 1, "Race," Writing, and Difference (Autumn, 1985), pp. 243-261*

Stoneman, P, *Charlotte Bronte: Writers and Their Work*. (Northcote: British Council, 2013).

Thormählen, M, *The Brontes and Religion* (Cambridge: Cambridge University Press, 1999).

Thormählen, M [ed], The Brontes in Context, (Cambridge: Cambridge University Press, 2014).

Watt, I, *The Rise of The Novel*, (London: Bodley Head, 2015).

Webb, I, *From Custom to Capital: The English Novel and the Industrial Revolution,* (London: Cornell Press, 1981).

Williams, R, *The Novel from Dickens to Lawrence* (London: Chatto & Windus, 1984).

Tony Cliff on the British Labour Party.

Starting point Lenin: The Labour Party is a 'capitalist worker's party' which has 'duped' the proletariat out of the fulfilment of its 'world historic mission' [Engels [to create socialism. and is therefore 'an organization of the bourgeois'. It tries to unite two contradictory forces 'the Nation' and 'the proletariat' which is international

Tony Cliff developed a model to explain the British Labour Party.:

- .'Reformist consciousness' = 1. Ideology of the ruling class vs 2. the experience of everyday exploitation where the goal is 'neither fish nor fowl' Cliff
- 'concentrated economics' 'born out of the bowls of the T.U.C. after a defeat in the class struggle, but nevertheless a step forward for the British working class.

Tripartite strata. There is no neutral ground in capitalism, we are in a condition of the ebb and flow of class conflict. The state is an 'instrument of class rule'

1. **Political expression of the trade union bureaucracy.** They act as in the embodiment of trade union consciousness in a crystalized form. On one hand, they negotiate deals with the bourgeois on the other they must sell those arguments to the rank and file.
2. **The problem of false consciousness:**

Marx *Preface to a Contribution to Political Economy*

'a distinction has to be made between the material conditions of production…and the legal, philosophical, aesthetic – in a word ideological-

forms in which men become conscious of [social] conflict and [how they] fight it out.'

So, although Reformists may be sincere but there is a gap between how things are

1.'class conflict' and 2. the Labour Party. i.e. the Labour Party does not reflect without ideological distortion the objective material conditions of British capitalism.

3. **A technical division of labour.**

a) The trade union bureaucracy is 'ONCE REMOVED from the class struggle because of its role in negotiating between he bosses and workers . They are a upper strata of the working class who interact with the state on the side of usually the bourgeoisie b) The Labour Party are 'TWICE REMOVED' they seek to represent the working class **1** they must appeal to the 'atomized' worker in the polling booth rather than the 'collective' working class in struggle 2) as a *'party standing above trade unionism'* they seek non-union votes.

Karl Marx: Hegel fell into the illusion of conceiving the real as the product of thought, the real subject retains its autonomous existence outside the head'.

Rosa Luxemburg 'The struggle for reforms are the means, the social revolution its goal.

Trotsky 'The Question of all questions' = answer is 'the revolutionary vanguard party'. It must lead the masses from the depths of capitalism to a new dawn for humanity, we may call this Communism.

www.ingramcontent.com/pod-product-compliance
Lightning Source LLC
Chambersburg PA
CBHW022156080426
42734CB00006B/454